Picture Framing
for the first time®

Picture Framing
for the first time®

By

Lee Bartholomew

Sterling Publishing Co., Inc. New York
A Sterling/Chapelle Book

Chapelle, Ltd.:
Jo Packham
Sara Toliver
Cindy Stoeckl

Editor: Ray Cornia
Art Director: Karla Haberstich
Copy Editor: Marilyn Goff
Photographers: Ryne Hazen and Kevin Dilley for Hazen Photography
Photo Stylists: Connie Duran and Suzy Skadburg
Graphic Illustrator: Kim Taylor

Staff: Kelly Ashkettle, Areta Bingham, Donna Chambers,
  Emily Frandsen, Lana Hall, Mackenzie Johnson, Susan Jorgensen,
  Jennifer Luman, Mellissa Maynard, Barbara Milburn, Lecia Monsen,
  Linda Venditti, Desirée Wybrow

If you have any questions or comments, please contact:
Chapelle, Ltd., Inc., P.O. Box 9252, Ogden, UT 84409
  (801) 621-2777 • (801) 621-2788 Fax
  e-mail: chapelle@chappelleltd.com
  web sites: www.chapelleltd.com
          www.rubyandbegonia.com

Library of Congress Cataloging-in-Publication Data available

10 9 8 7 6 5 4 3 2 1

Published by Sterling Publishing Co., Inc.
387 Park Avenue South, New York, NY 10016
©2004 by Lee Bartholomew
Distributed in Canada by Sterling Publishing
c/o Canadian Manda Group, One Atlantic Avenue, Suite 105
Toronto, Ontario, Canada M6K 3E7
Distributed in Great Britain by Chrysalis Books
64 Brewery Road, London N7 9NT, England
Distributed in Australia by Capricorn Link (Australia) Pty. Ltd.
P.O. Box 704, Windsor, NSW 2756, Australia
Printed in China
All Rights Reserved

Sterling ISBN 1-4027-0634-0

Introduction

Many people have, at one time or another, attempted to frame a picture. Some of these attempts have resulted in a wonderful product, others are not so satisfying. However, with proper instruction and a little practice, anyone can become proficient at making a perfect picture frame. This book will demonstrate many procedures commonly used by both hobbyists and professional framers. Instructions are provided for various framing methods to match your budget, availability of tools, and the requirements of the project.

Pictured here is one of my first frames. Like many first-timers, my first frame was a barn-wood frame with a crude but ingenious method of joinery. I made this piece as a teenager and since that time, I have learned a great deal. I hope that by sharing some of these things, your learning process as a frame builder will be simplified.

How to Use this Book

This book is designed as a step-by-step guide for basic picture framing. While there are no extraordinary skills needed to follow the instructions in this book, a basic knowledge of and access to woodworking tools and materials will be requisite.

The framing Basics section of the book will give a general overview of framing terms, tools, and materials. Detailed framing instructions will be provided in the Basic Techniques and Project sections of the book.

Each of the Technique projects in the book teaches new framing skills. Successively, they build upon each other to provide a basic understanding of frame making. There are photos and illustrations showing the tools and materials needed to properly construct a professional-looking frame. You will also find formulas and diagrams that will help you understand the basic math needed to calculate the proper cuts for both matting and framing materials.

The best thing about this book is that there are lots of pictures. I am a firm believer that we are inspired to do great things by what we see around us. So I have gathered some of my favorite projects together to show what can be done. Browse through the framing examples throughout this book, and apply the ideas to your own projects.

Although experimenting can make a project more expensive with every mistake, I encourage using different elements of design and new ideas to create beautiful, original pieces of framing artwork.

Table of Contents

Section 1:
Framing Basics—8

Section 2:
Basic Techniques—26

Section 4:
Dynamic Presentations—104

Section 1: Framing Basics

Basic Framing Tools

Backsaw (very sharp) and miter box

Cleaning rags

Drill bits

Hammer

Hand-held glass cutter

Hand-held mat cutter and extra blades

Hard-lead pencil, 3H or harder

Kneaded eraser

Large T-square, with nonslip cork or rubber back

Metal ruler, with nonslip cork or rubber back

Needle-nosed pliers

Nonslip-grip cloth gloves

Paintbrush

Paper towels

Power drill

Safety glasses

Screwdrivers

Small T-square

Squeeze Clamp(s)

Strap clamp

Table (very sturdy and flat at least 5' x 3')

Tape measure

Utility knife and extra blades

Wire cutters

It is difficult for me to suggest tools for a beginning frame builder. Some people are highly cost conscious and would prefer not to invest in expensive tools. While it is unnecessary to purchase top-of-the-line tools, good quality tools are a must.

With this in mind, I have attempted to divide my tool list into two parts: Basic Tools—these are tools that are definitely needed, and Professional Tools—

Hammer   Drill bits   Drill   Screwdrivers   Wire cutters   Paintbrush   Hard-lead pencil

these are tools, used for the projects in this book, that make the job easier and faster, but which might cost more than the hobby frame builder is able to justify when first beginning. As framing projects become larger, more detailed, or more numerous, these optional tools quickly become required tools.

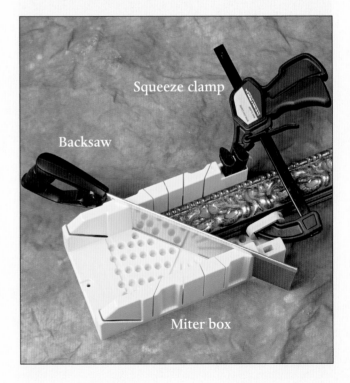

Squeeze clamp   Backsaw   Miter box

Another point worth carefully considering is the size and type of framing to be done. Take a photographer who shoots 35mm film. Maximum size for finished prints would probably be 16" x 20". Since the photographs might be shown together, the photographer may wish to frame all the photographs alike with a neutral colored mat and simple black frame. Under these circumstances the basic tools would work very well because the resulting frames would be quite small and manageable. Required tabletop workspace would be minimal.

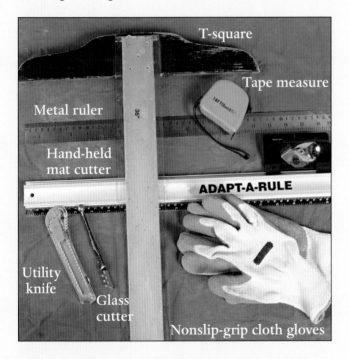

On the other hand, an oil painter who regularly paints large canvases would need a larger work area for framing and he may need more sophisticated tools just to handle the larger frames he is required to make to properly display his paintings.

Time is another factor to consider. A professional-grade tool is expensive, but it often saves a great amount of time and cuts down on costly mistakes because it is usually easier to use. The time savings can also help those who sell their work appear to be more professional. Quick turnaround from time of sale to delivery of the product is important when promoting a professional image and setting the stage for subsequent sales.

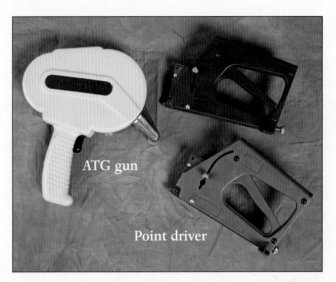

An ATG gun and point drivers are relatively inexpensive and really make frame finishing quick and easy. Because they make such a profound difference in the speed and quality of the framing process, some frame builders feel that these tools are not optional for serious framing projects.

By following the directions in this book, you will learn how to use these tools and decide for yourself how they will work for your framing projects.

Professional Tools

90° corner clamp

Agate burnishing stone

ATG Tape gun

Craft knife and replacement blades

Dust cover

Ear protection

Glass-breaking pliers, curved rubber nose preferred

Pneumatic brad or staple gun

Point driver

Power miter saw (sharp)

Tabletop mat cutter

Professional tools could be defined as tools which are not absolutely necessary in order to do the job of framing. If you were to visit several frame shops, you would certainly find tools that are not listed in this book. Tools such as a double miter saw, computerized mat cutters, dry-mount presses, etc. These tools, while valuable, are very specialized or tied to techniques not addressed in this book.

Since this is a first-time framing book, I have strived to simplify all aspects of the book—including a listing of framing tools. As your skill in framing increases, you will find the tools that support your vision as to what the perfect frame should be and how it should be built. My purpose in giving a list of tools is to get you started properly and help you achieve some successful framing projects.

Power miter saw

Pneumatic staple gun

Craft knife

Glass-breaking pliers

Agate burnishing stone

90° corner clamp

Basic Materials

Backing paper (kraft paper)

Brads or staples, 1"

Braided wire

Cardboard, for use as a cutting surface

Colored nail-hole filler, nonhardening

Double-sided tape

D-strap hanger

Fabric hinging tape

Finish nails (refer to projects for specific size)

Florist tape

Foam-core backing

Frame molding

Framing tape

Gummed Japanese rice paper

Rubber or felt bumpers

Sandpaper, 180-grit

Sawtooth picture hanger

Selected mat board

Spray adhesive

Touch-up colored pens, rottenstone, filler, or paint

Wood filler

Wood glue

If giving a basic list of tools was difficult, trying to identify some basic materials is almost impossible. Every different style of frame will call for a new type of filler, touch-up color, or antiquing material. Here, I have made up a list that gives the frame builder a general idea of what to look for when constructing and finishing a frame.

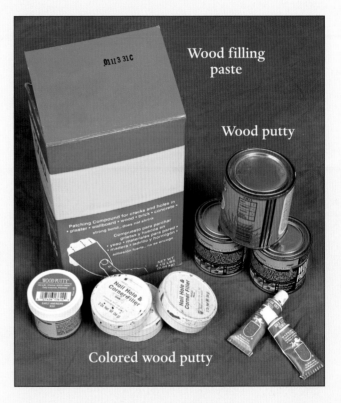

Wood filling paste

Wood putty

Colored wood putty

Some materials, like wood filler, come in various forms. The wood filler that works perfectly for one application may not work properly for the next project. It is important to learn how each product performs in various situations. Sometimes a particular brand will perform differently than that of a competitor. When using a new product or a different brand of a familiar product, be careful to thoroughly read the manufacturer's instructions.

Touch-up colored pens

Types of Frames

Ready-made Frames

Ready-made frames are available in a wide variety of finishes and sizes. If your picture project fits into one of these frames, and if you can find a style that suits you, it is an inexpensive alternative to a custom-built frame. Listed are some of the more common sizes:

4" x 6"	11" x 14"	24" x 30"
5" x 7"	12" x 16"	24" x 36"
6" x 8"	14" x 18"	30" x 40"
8" x 10"	16" x 20"	32" x 40"
8½" x 11"	18" x 24"	36" x 48"
9" x 12"	20" x 24"	40" x 60"
10" x 13"	22" x 28"	

Sectional Frames

Sectional frames are basically an unassembled type of ready-made frame. They come in both metal and wood and are available in a variety of finishes. You simply choose two different packs containing the appropriate sizes of precut molding. Joining the molding is simple, using the enclosed hardware.

Hardware Store Molding Frames

Most hardware stores sell premilled wooden molding. This molding makes excellent framing material. Selection of profiles is typically limited at a hardware store so try to choose one with a design that enhances the picture and wide enough to include a precut rabbet. The advantage to this material is that it is usually unfinished so you are not paying for that feature. You can then finish it as you desire and make a truly unique and personalized frame.

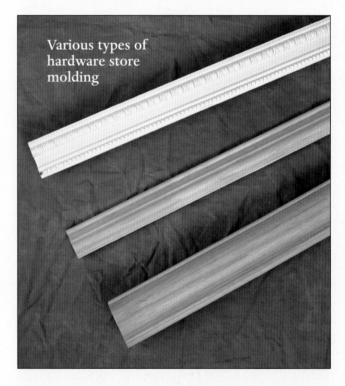

Various types of hardware store molding

Because it is relatively inexpensive, hardware store molding is perfect for the beginning frame builder to use while learning. It is perfect for using with new finishes or building techniques. Some people like picture frames to match the trim in one or more of the rooms in their houses. This decorating touch is especially charming when used with mirrors.

Prefinished Wooden Frame Molding

This is the type of material that most people think of when they see a framed picture. There are many colors and styles and the molding is made specifically for mounting pictures complete with mat and a glazing cover. It is easy to select the frame because you can place a sample section of the molding on your picture at a frame store and get a good idea of how it will look once it is finished.

Of course, prefinished frame molding comes with a price—literally. Depending on the style selected, it can be costly; however, if it sets off the picture properly, it is money well spent. For those wishing to purchase prefinished frame molding so they can craft their own frames, it is wise to shop around. Some frame stores cater to the independent frame builder better than do others. In some cases, it is possible to purchase prefinished frame molding at a wholesale price; however, this may involve the use of a resale number which many independent frame builders do not have.

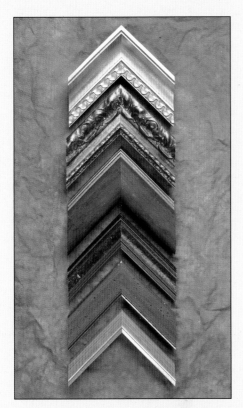

Barn-wood Frames

Frames made of weathered barn wood have always been popular for use with artwork having a rustic flair. Most of the time, this material must be cut and shaped with a table saw before the framer can properly handle it. Care must be taken so the wood that touches the artwork is properly sealed to keep out mildew, mold, and various other staining agents inherent in the wood.

On the plus side, sloppy joints, exposed nails, and crooked mountings only seem to add to the charm of a barn-wood frame. On the other hand, a well-crafted frame coupled with the proper mat and appropriately selected piece of art can produce something that can only be described as elegant.

Molding Length Calculator

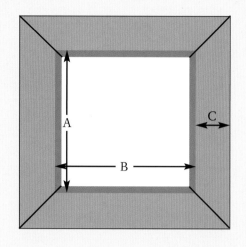

United Inches	Molding Width									
	½"	1"	1½"	2"	2½"	3"	3½"	4"	4½"	5"
10	26	30	34	38	42	46	50	54	58	62
12	30	34	38	42	46	50	54	58	62	66
14	34	38	42	46	50	54	58	62	66	70
16	38	42	46	50	54	58	62	66	70	74
18	42	46	50	54	58	62	66	70	74	78
20	46	50	54	58	62	66	70	74	78	82
22	50	54	58	62	66	70	74	78	82	86
24	54	58	62	66	70	74	78	82	86	90
26	58	62	66	70	74	78	82	86	90	94
28	62	66	70	74	78	82	86	90	94	98
30	66	70	74	78	82	86	90	94	98	102
32	70	74	78	82	86	90	94	98	102	106
34	74	78	82	86	90	94	98	102	106	110
36	78	82	86	90	94	98	102	106	110	114
38	82	86	90	94	98	102	106	110	114	118
40	86	90	94	98	102	106	110	114	118	122
42	90	94	98	102	106	110	114	118	122	126
44	94	98	102	106	110	114	118	122	126	130
46	98	102	106	110	114	118	122	126	130	134
48	102	106	110	114	118	122	126	130	134	138
50	106	110	114	118	122	126	130	134	138	142
52	110	114	118	122	126	130	134	138	142	146
54	114	118	122	126	130	134	138	142	146	150
56	118	122	126	130	134	138	142	146	150	154
58	122	126	130	134	138	142	146	150	154	158
60	126	130	134	138	142	146	150	154	158	162
62	130	134	138	142	146	150	154	158	162	166
64	134	138	142	146	150	154	158	162	166	170
66	138	142	146	150	154	158	162	166	170	174
68	142	146	150	154	158	162	166	170	174	178
70	146	150	154	158	162	166	170	174	178	182
72	150	154	158	162	166	170	174	178	182	186
74	154	158	162	166	170	174	178	182	186	190
76	158	162	166	170	174	178	182	186	190	194
78	162	166	170	174	178	182	186	190	194	198
80	166	170	174	178	182	186	190	194	198	202

The purpose of the Molding Length Calculator is to make a rough calculation of how much molding material you will need for your framing project. Once you have determined the dimensions of your frame package (see page 17), you imagine placing the frame on its face. Take the width plus the height of the frame window (A plus B) in inches. This number becomes the "united inches" used in the left-hand column.

Determine the width of the molding from the rabbet to the edge of the frame (C).

Where the two columns meet, is the number of inches of molding needed to frame your artwork.

For example, if the width of the frame window is 20" and the height is 18", then the united inches number would be 38, or 38". If you choose a molding that is 3" wide, then you will need 102" of molding for your project.

To each dimension, 2" has been added for cutting waste. Check to insure that the uncut stick length of the molding will accommodate the needed frame side measurements.

Frame Package

Over the years as I have taught other people to frame, I found it was easiest to break the framing process into three components. First, is the glazing, mat, artwork, and backing which comprises a "frame package." This in turn, fits into the second component, the frame.

Once the frame package is secure in the frame, the final component consisting of the finishing paper and hanging system are installed and the project is complete.

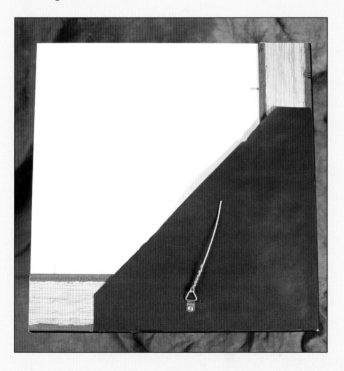

Mat Boards

The most important thing about choosing a mat board is not color, size, or texture, but quality. Most mats available to consumers today are labeled "acid free." This is a very meaningless label, as many of these mats are replete with acid, lignin, nitrogen dioxide, and other damaging chemicals and pollutants. The manufacturers add a buffering compound such as calcium bicarbonate to counteract the effects of the acids; however, these compounds can become unbalanced over time. On an average, these well-meaning mats will only retain their true color for several months and will lose their neutral ph after approximately five years.

There are a few brands of mat boards available that are of exceptional quality. Look for either 100% cotton rag or acid- and lignin-free alpha-cellulose conservation boards. These mats will be roughly twice as expensive as the alternative, but the better quality will pay off in a very short time. On the other hand, some framed pieces are not intended to last permanently. The less expensive mats may be perfectly adequate for these projects.

Backing Material

In the past, many types of material such as cardboard and fiberboard have been used as backing for framed pieces. Most of these materials were not ideal for that application. The modern foam-core backing has been a boon for framing. It resists moisture, is acid-free, and is lighter which helps with the overall framed-package weight. Just as with mat material, the more-expensive archival foam-core backing is superior to cheaper alternatives.

Glazing

There are many types of prewashed annealed glass available to picture framers. Following is a brief glass overview:

Single- and/or double-strength clear glass. This glass is inexpensive and provides good image clarity with slight color distortion. However, reflection can be a problem if not properly lit.

Nonglare glass. Make certain it is etched on just one side with the etched side out. Reflection is reduced but the image will become blurred when using three or more mats or when viewed at an angle.

Conservation clear UV protected glass. This glazing is great for posters and reproduction art that does not have a long viewing life. It blocks 97% of UV light, which is a major contributor to fading.

Conservation reflection-control UV protected glass. This is a better quality reflection-control glass with less blurring of the framed artwork. It also has the added UV protection.

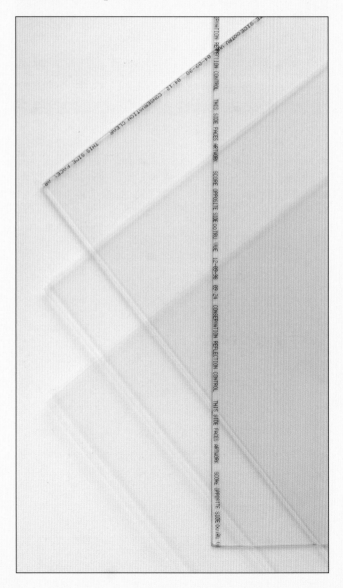

"**White**" **glass**. This optically clear glass does not distort, darken, or "green" images. Reflection can be a problem if not properly lit.

Antireflection glass. Some brands eliminate glare almost completely. They are quite expensive and most of them are porous and require special handling and cleaning. It can even be used on deep shadow boxes with excellent clarity.

Museum glass. This optically clear UV protected glass also offers the best antireflective qualities. It is very pricey, but well worth the cost.

Acrylic glazing. Optically clear, this shatter-resisting glazing, is available in reflection-control and UV-protection styles. It scratches easily and can warp in direct sunlight or if placed near heat sources. Do not use with pastels or charcoal drawings. Static builds up in the acrylic and attracts medium off of the substrate, causing damage to the artwork and creating a hazy look on the glazing.

Frame Finishing

Backing Paper (dust cover)

While backing paper is not necessary, it makes the job look more finished and professional. It also keeps dirt, and moisture away from the frame package. For the professional frame builder, it provides an excellent surface to place a sticker informing the owner of the artwork where the frame was built.

Kraft paper works well for this application; however, museums use a tougher material.

Hanging Hardware

There are numerous methods for hanging framed artwork. I have selected two methods which should work for most framing projects. The first is the saw-tooth hanger. This is used with lightweight frames and is very easy to install.

The second hanging method selected is the D-strap and braided-wire system. This is also simple to install and by adding heavier D-straps and more strands of wire, it is possible to hang very heavy pieces. D-straps can also be mounted vertically on the frame and placed directly on hanging hooks.

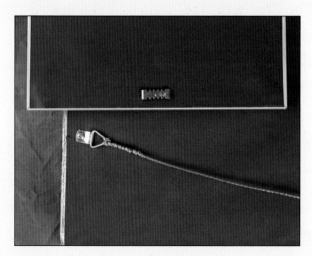

Selecting a Frame

I think that we have all seen a frame that makes the artwork look cheap and poorly done. On the other hand, there are frames far more interesting than the artwork. Framing material comes in as many finishes and profiles as it is imaginable for us to comprehend. With so many choices available, it is often mind boggling to choose the proper frame for one picture.

The first thing to understand in choosing the correct frame is that all things are relative to that which they can be compared. Even the environment in which the finished piece is to be displayed needs to be addressed. Yes, it is necessary to match the furnishings of a room. However, if the piece is to be sold to an unknown buyer, then the framing must be more generic in its color and style.

In my store, I have the chance to talk to people about beautiful framing daily. Before selling them just any frame, I try to familiarize them with the elements that constitute proper balance and presentation in framing. I have broken these elements into four categories:

> Texture
> Color and intensity
> Mass or visual weight
> Style

Texture

Texture deals with the surfaces of the picture and the frame. A roughly painted oil painting with a glossy damar varnish has a different texture than the same painting painted in matte acrylic or gouache. A traditional watercolor has a very natural soft surface, and a pastel is soft to the extreme. A graphic poster usually has a very smooth clean appearance.

Subject matter also influences the texture of the frame. A child's drawing is well presented in a smooth, matte painted frame. A print or poster is a reproduction of the original medium, so an impressionistic oil painting will be well presented in a frame with a little more texture than a slick framed print.

Texture in a frame includes both pattern and layering of color. Light scrapes across the surface of an ornate frame breaks up the surface and adds textural interest. The same-sized frame in a smooth simple profile might appear larger or more massive simply because there is not as much going on visually. Conversely, there might also be a time when an ornate frame might give a sense of undesirable "busyness."

When using a mat inside of the frame, it can act as a "buffer zone" between the artwork and the frame. As long as the mat goes well with the frame, artwork, and style that you are trying to achieve, your frame choice is much less important. Much of choosing a frame comes with practice and development of the artistic eye. Trust your instincts. Also, trust the instincts of those around you. Good design is apparent to most people, they just do not always know how to best implement it.

Color and Intensity

There are many books on color theory, and artists and designers have devoted their entire adult lives trying to fully understand the relationship between different colors. We have all seen color charts and been taught about the primary colors. This is wonderful information to have; however, not many of us possess the knowledge necessary to understand completely the relationship of what "goes" together. I have some simple little tricks that seem to help:

• Look at the color that predominantly borders the entire piece.

• If there is an even distribution of warm and cool tones, choose the color that works best with the bottom third of the image (especially in a still life or landscape).

• Choose a predominant color from the piece, add a little gray in the coloring of the mat to tone it down slightly. This tends to make the painting illuminate in the frame.

- Dark frames can offer more flexibility on artwork with rich, saturated colors.

- Gold frames are great on warm pieces while silver is best used on midtoned to cool-colored artwork.

I have learned that almost every rule has its exception. If you try something and it doesn't work, try what you do not think would work, it may surprise you. With the proper knowledge and experience, every rule of balance and proportion can be twisted or broken. After you master the traditional rules of color, try new things, because once again, you might like it.

Mass or Visual Weight

Have you ever seen a frame and you said, "That frame is too big." Often, size has very little to do with the way that frames can overpower the artwork.

One of my favorite framing examples is a small painting of two trees. I placed a 4"-wide dark wood frame on it. Under most conventional thinking, that

would be way too much, but it looks wonderful. I have also framed a 36"-square landscape in a gilded silver leaf frame, with a deep 1"-wide rabbet and it worked even better than I planned. So, the rule of large painting, large frame; small painting, small frame does not always apply.

The purpose of this list of "rules" is not to give you a complete guide to perfect frame design; but it is given so that you consciously think about how things go together. Mass is the most relative portion of frame design. Look closely at each piece individually, avoid using the same frame on everything; it will only work if you are framing the same print more than once.

Style

The frame should reflect as many elements of the piece as possible. A piece with large swirling lines would go well in a curved profile frame. Possibly the same piece could fit with an ornamental frame with a similarity in its design and presentation. Look for elements in each piece and each molding, and make them work well together.

There are many conventions that can be broken in the category of style. I am not an advocate of "purist framing," when the frame must be from the proper era or location for a particular piece. We live in a very conglomerated society today; thus, many of our frame choices may reflect our melting-pot thinking. I once framed an abstract landscape in an ornate frame from the Czech Republic. I also framed an 18th century engraving in a modern matte black frame with a 6" mat. Play with the conventions of framing to distort the way in which things are perceived. From abstract to neoclassical and from antique to modern, simply find things that are beautiful when placed together.

Selecting an Appropriate Mat

As mentioned on page 17, the most important thing about choosing a mat for your frame package is not color, size, or texture, but quality. Look for either 100% cotton rag or acid- and lignin-free alpha-cellulose conservation boards.

When choosing mats, you can refer to the rules that I use for choosing a frame. In addition, I will give some other factors to consider when making mat selections:

• The mat that touches the picture is called the transitional mat. It should address the color that is most prevalent all the way around the exterior of the piece.

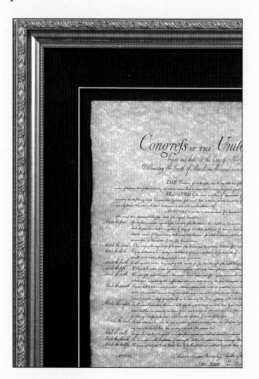

• If there is an equal distribution of warm and cool tones in the piece, your mats should be chosen to match the bottom third of the piece.

• Avoid choosing a mat that is more color saturated or a combination of mats that has more contrast than contained in the picture.

• When using three mats, the center mat is called the accent mat. It should be used to pull subtle accents from the interior of the piece. Used correctly, the accent mat can help the viewer's eye travel uninhibited throughout the piece without being distracted by the matting and framing.

• If using a very strong color as an accent (center) mat, you can lessen the weight of it by decreasing the reveal, or exposed area, of that mat.

- The top mat must be much more exact in color and value than anything else in the frame. It should be chosen carefully, with attention given to accenting the artwork best. The color should be slightly muted, to allow the artwork to have more strength.

- If using a darker or more saturated mat color for your top mat, more than one mat is often necessary to give a richer look and to address more of what is going on in the picture.

- A wider top mat can often provide a simpler look by creating less visual detail close to the image.

- If the original artwork being framed is for resale, it is not wise to spend much for the mat or the frame. Chances are the new owner will want to reframe the piece to fit in with the decor of the room where it will be placed. Oftentimes the best solution is a white to off-white mat to match the color of the paper or substrate or the lightest white in the picture. This same general look is also achieved using black or gray mats. The single mat presentation gives a contemporary look and is acceptable for most galleries and museums. Should the frame be damaged through transportation or handling, it will not be a great loss.

Section 2: Basic Techniques

1
Technique

What you need to get started:

Tools:
- Basic framing tools (see pages 10–11)

Materials:
- Oil or acrylic painting on fiberboard
- Rags or paper towels
- Small finish nails
- Wood glue
- Wood sectional frame

How do I assemble a wood sectional frame?

Wood sectional frames are designed to be easy to assemble and use. They are perfect for the beginning frame builder.

Wood Framed Painting

Activity concepts: Constructing wood sectional frame, sawtooth hanger.

Here's how:

1. Purchase two packages of sectional molding based on the size of your project. For example, for a 8" x 6" frame, choose one 8" and one 6" package.

2. Open the packages carefully to avoid marring surface of the frame. Lay out frame pieces as they will fit together face up on clean work surface.

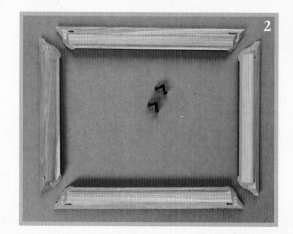

NOTE: You will find two "I" shaped plastic thumbnail inserts in each package, DO NOT DISCARD.

This abstract landscape is inexpensively framed in an oak sectional frame. Size: 7" x 9½"

3. Glue the two edges of one corner. Insert plastic thumbnail into proper slots and push molding pieces together to form frame corner.

4. Repeat assembly process on the remaining three corners.

5. Wipe off excess glue with rag or paper towel and allow glue to dry.

Frame finishing

1. Insert painting into frame and secure with small finish nails. Exact nail size is not important.

Attaching a sawtooth hanger

1. Install sawtooth hanger on back of frame, following package instructions.

   NOTE: *Since it is sometimes difficult to hold the saw-tooth hanger onto the frame while hammering, use needle-nosed pliers or tweezers to hold it in place.*

How do I assemble a metal sectional frame?

Metal sectional frames are easy to assemble and give a nice contemporary look to any picture.

Metal Framed Poster

Activity concepts: Constructing metal sectional frame, spray-mounting onto foam-core backing, cutting glass, and attaching wire hanger .

Here's how:

1. Purchase two packages of metal sectional molding based on the size of your project. For example, for a 20" x 10" frame, choose one 20" and one 10" package.

2. Open packages carefully to avoid marring the surface of the frame.
   NOTE: You will find four "L" shaped faceplates (with screws) and four back plates. You will also find a hanging system.

3. Lay out frame pieces as they will fit together face down on a hard clean work surface.

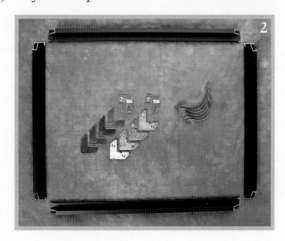

What you need to get started:

Tools:
- Basic framing tools (see pages 10–11)
- Glass pliers

Materials:
- Ammonia-free nonstreaking glass cleaner
- Florist tape
- Foam-core backing
- Glass
- Lint-free cloths or paper towel
- Mat, precut to fit frame
- Metal sectional frame
- Newspaper
- Poster for framing
- Slipsheet
- Spray adhesive

NOTE: One advantage to metal sectional frames is that they can usually be custom cut to fit an odd-sized picture. However, it is advisable to have someone in a frame shop, using the proper saw and blade, do this type of cut.

31

This reproduction print maintains a clean classic presentation in this black metal sectional frame. Size: 11¼" x 14¼"

4. Place one faceplate and one back plate together, then slide plates into slot at back of one long frame section.

5. Slide one short frame section into place and secure with screws.

   NOTE: *It is important that these frame sections line up perfectly and that they are held securely together while tightening.*

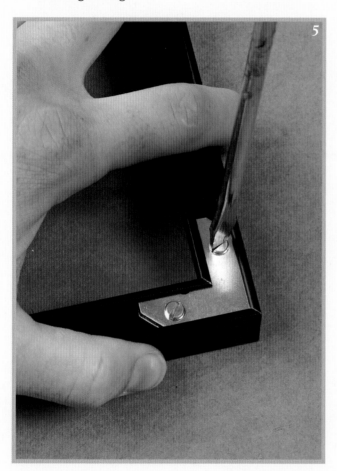

6. Repeat process on the next corner. Once the first two corners are finished, the assembled "frame package" (glazing, poster, and backing) can be inserted.

   NOTE: *Stop here and prepare "frame package," following instructions for "Adhering paper based artwork onto backing material," above right.*

Adhering paper-based artwork onto backing material

Spray-mounting the artwork onto foam-core backing is the quickest but most invasive and damaging method of attachment. This system works well for pieces that only need to last a few years. The inexpensive backing is fine for this type of mounting.

1. Cut a piece of backing 2"–4" larger than the size of the frame.

2. Lay out two separate sections of newspaper for "groundcloths." Place backing in center of one paper section and mark. Remove backing. Center poster in marks made for backing so poster will be located in proper position under backing and mark poster position.

3. Place poster face down on second groundcloth. Place the backing face up next to the poster on same groundcloth.

4. Evenly spray back of poster and front-center section of backing with adhesive, following manufacturer's instructions.

5. Allow both sprayed surfaces to dry for approximately one minute.

6. Place poster face down in proper position on the first groundcloth.

7. Place backing face down onto back of poster making certain poster remains in proper position.

8. Turn backing face up and smooth poster with a clean soft cloth.
   NOTE: *The newspaper may stick to the sprayed area on the backing, but it can be easily removed. If ink*

from the newspaper sticks to the backing, it will not matter because this area will be covered with the mat.

9. Lay mat in position over mounted piece, then trim backing to the edge of mat, using metal ruler and utility knife or mat cutter.

Cutting glass

Most framing projects use glass to protect the item being framed. While many people are intimidated by the thought of cutting glass, given the proper tools, it is really quite easy to do.

There are many types of glass available: annealed, tempered, and laminated glass. Framers use annealed glass because it is the only type of glass that can be cut after production. Refer to Glazing on pages 18–19. The others are made to size and will shatter or star-chip if you try to score and cut them.

The cutting process involves scoring the glass, using a small hand-held glass scorer and a nonslip straightedge as a guide. This creates a scratch in the surface of the glass, and actually changes the way that the molecules attach to each other throughout the thickness of the glass along the scored line. The glass should be run and broken immediately as the glass can actually regain some of its strength with time and as a result give a poor uneven break. Here is how it is done:

1. Place a piece of mat board or clean cardboard on a raised surface with a sturdy straight side such as a countertop or a table.

2. Put on safety glasses. This is important because although it is not probable, it is possible for glass splinters to fly up into your face.

3. Wearing gloves with nonslip rubber grips, place glass on the prepared surface.

4. Measure height or width of desired cut with a tape measure. Place a nonslip T-square or metal ruler on the measuring point and hold in place.

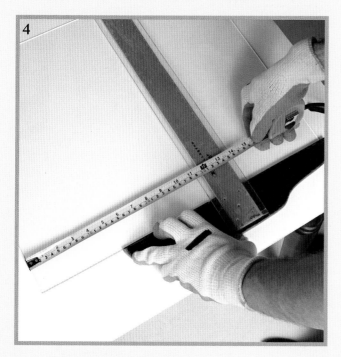

NOTE: A T-square is easier to use than a metal ruler because you can place the "T" on the edge of the glass and get a true 90° cut that will be perpendicular to the adjoining edge with only one measurement. If you cannot find a T-square with a cork back, place a strip of electrician's friction tape on the back of a metal T-square.

5. Apply firm pressure on the T-square to keep it from slipping. Place the tip of the glass scorer (roller) against the T-square and ⅛" in from the end that is opposite you.
NOTE: UV protected glass can usually be cut from only one side. The manufacturer marks it with instructions.

6. Apply even pressure to the scorer as you pull it toward you. You should hear an even "nails on the chalkboard" sound. If you hear or see skips in the score, replace or lubricate the scorer. Pull the scorer to within ⅛" of the end closest to you.
NOTE: You must cut the glass from one edge to the other. You cannot take a "section" from the glass and leave an L-shape in the original glass piece.

7. Turn the sheet of glass, with the waste side out, so that the scored line is directly over the edge of the work surface for its entire length.

8 Grasp in the middle of the waste side firmly and while holding the other side tightly against the table, press down on the waste side. The score should break along the entire length of glass all at once.

8a

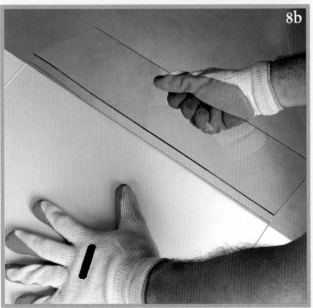

8b

9. If that method does not appeal to you, purchase some glass-breaking pliers. With pliers, simply straddle the score with the pliers and squeeze.
NOTE: When working with a thicker piece of glass, it might be necessary to "run" the score first. To do this, just hold the glass flat with the waste side extended past the table. Tap the underneath side of the glass with the ball on the end of the glass cutter, you will see a crack spreading underneath the score. When the score has been completely run, it will be easy to make the break properly.

10. Repeat Steps 4–9 to cut the other dimension.

11. If you have any areas that did not break properly, just use the "teeth" on the roller end of the scorer to "bite" the glass chips off.
NOTE: Some people advocate rounding off the sharp edges of the glass for safety sake. There are many ways to do this, the easiest is to sand the edges with 150-grit sandpaper installed on a sanding block. The downside is that whatever method is used, dust will need to be cleaned off the glass. Even if you round off the edges, there may still be some sharp areas left. The best solution is to always be cautious when handling glass.

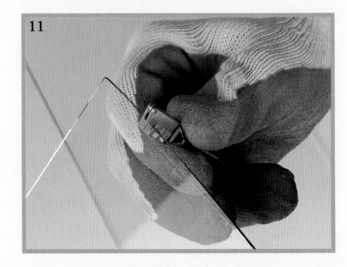

11

Cleaning glass

Hopefully you purchased prewashed glass and have only handled it with gloves. If so, just blow off the glass and move on to Frame finishing. If not, follow these instructions:

1. Wear gloves to clean glass. Most framing injuries to the hands come when cleaning glass.

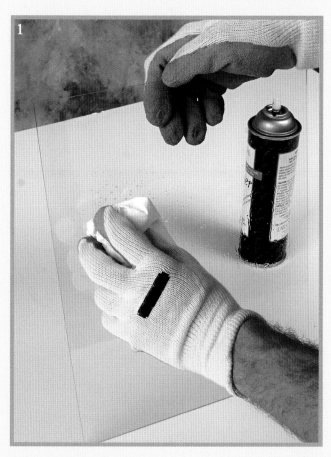

2. Always brush or blow off glass before cleaning.

3. Using a soft clean cloth or lint-free paper towel, clean glass with ammonia-free, nonstreaking glass cleaner. Ammonia can cause major problems with some types of framed artwork.

4. Inspect cleaned glass in good lighting to make certain all streaks have been removed.

Frame finishing

1. Insert frame package into frame and fasten the last brackets into position.

2. Place both remaining corner brackets into the last frame section, then slide frame section into place.

3. Tighten all screws.

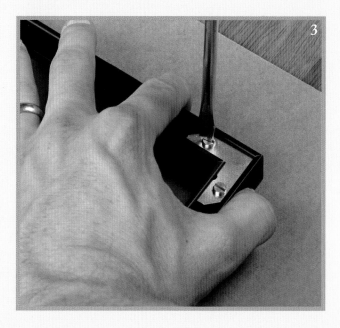

4. Install spring clips to keep frame package tightly in place.

NOTE: Wear safety glasses for installing and removing spring clips. They can spring directly at your eyes if they slip.

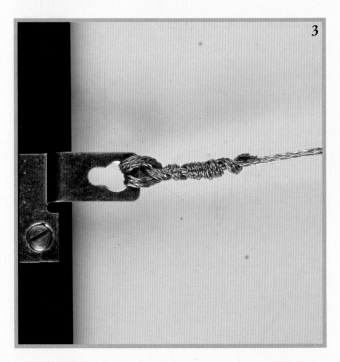

5. Install hanger, following the manufacturer's instructions.

Attaching braided picture wire

1. Measure and cut braided wire to width of frame plus 8". Pull wire through both D-strap hangers.

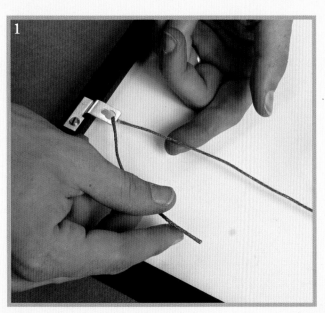

2. Tie knots in wire. The wire should be taut so that when the picture is hung, the D-straps will be about 1"–2" below the hanging hook attached to the wall.

3. Bend wire tail around wire.

4. Wrap florist tape (available at craft stores) around the ends of the wire to secure in place.

How can I make a frame from hardware store wooden molding?

Hardware store wooden molding is inexpensive but limited in variety of design. It can, however, be finished to match the other design features in a room. It is the perfect material to help you develop your framing skills.

Framed Certificate

Activity concepts: Calculating molding length, calculating size of frame, cutting frame with backsaw and miter box, gluing frame, use of strap clamp, nail joining, filling holes and cracks with wood filler, finishing frame with stain and varnish, applying paper backing, installing a D-strap and wire hanger.

Here's how:

Assembling the frame package

NOTE: For this project the frame package consists of the cover glass, mat, and certificate (business license).

1. Cut glass to same size as mat. Refer to Cutting glass on pages 34–36.

2. Lay the mat on the work table.

3. Place the certificate face down on newspaper and evenly spray with adhesive.

What you need to get started:

Tools:
- Basic framing tools (see pages 10–11)

Materials:
- Braided wire
- Certificate for framing
- Double-sided tape
- D-strap hanger
- Finish nails
- Glass
- Kraft paper
- Mat, precut to fit certificate
- Newspaper
- Rags or paper towels
- Rubber or felt bumper dots
- Sandpaper, 180-grit
- Screws, sized for frame depth
- Spray adhesive
- Stain
- Varnish
- Wood filler
- Wood glue
- Wooden molding

Documents such as this yearly business license can be framed to give them greater visual appeal.
If properly done, it can be easily removed and replaced when needed. Size: 14⅛" x 9½"

4. Before adhesive dries, center certificate on mat and gently smooth into place.

Measuring the molding

NOTE: Selection of molding profiles is typically limited at a hardware store. Try to select one with a rabbet and with a design that looks good with the picture.

1. Make certain to purchase enough molding. Refer to Molding Length Calculator on page 16.

2. To determine how wide to cut frame, measure the width of "frame package," or "A".

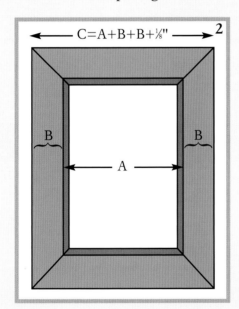

3. Measure the back of molding from the rabbet edge to the outside edge of molding, or "B," for both sides.

4. Add these two dimensions plus ⅛" for extra space in the frame for expansion of materials. This is the size that you will cut the outside, or "long side," of the molding "C" or C=A+B+B+⅛".

5. Repeat to determine the height of frame.

Cutting molding with a backsaw and a miter box

1. Attach miter box firmly to workbench. The miter box should not be so worn that the saw wobbles as you cut.

2. Place molding in the miter box with the rabbet facing away from you.

3. Clamp molding onto the side of miter box closest to you.

4. Support entire length of molding at the same height as miter box. If the piece of molding is long, it may be necessary to clamp or weight it down at the "loose" end.

5. Using a sharp backsaw, make the first 45° cut with shorter side of the miter toward rabbet part of molding. Remember, rabbet edge is the inside of the frame.

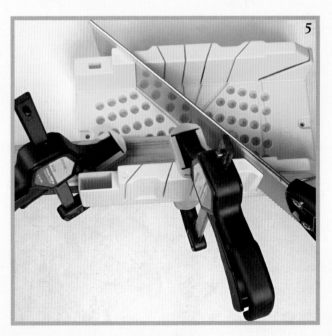

NOTE: A backsaw cuts best as you pull it toward you. Do not push it into the molding, rather focus on pulling the saw evenly toward you with slight downward pressure. Maintain a smooth flow to your movements to keep blade from grabbing and tearing.

6. When cut is completed, release clamps holding the molding.

7. Measure back edge of frame from the mitered end to the longest "C" dimension determined. Mark off and cut a long side of framing. By cutting a longer side first, you allow for possible mistakes. If you make a mistake, you can cut the molding down to make a smaller side.

8. Change backsaw in miter box to 45° in the other direction.

9. Align blade with the mark, then clamp molding firmly on both sides of blade. Keep in mind the waste side of the blade, so you don't cut off too much. Cut as described in Step 5 on page 41.

10. Repeat Steps 2–9 for the second long side.

11. Repeat Steps 2–9 for the two shorter sides.

12. To insure that opposite pieces are the exact length, place the pieces that are the same length back to back. If they are not exactly the same, trim a little off of the longer one until they are exactly the same length. Since trimming is very difficult, it is far easier to get it right the first time; so please, measure twice, cut once.

Gluing and joining the molding into a frame

Strap clamps are available at any large hardware store, and are very useful when joining frames, especially those having more than four sides. It works by wrapping a strap through multiple corner brackets all around the frame. The advantage to this type of joining is that you can join all sides simultaneously. The disadvantage is that on most frames you must allow the glued corners to fully dry before attempting to fortify the joins with nails, brads, or staples.

1. Lay out frame pieces face up on flat surface. Leave corners with a slight gap.

2. Position strap clamp and corner brackets loosely around frame.

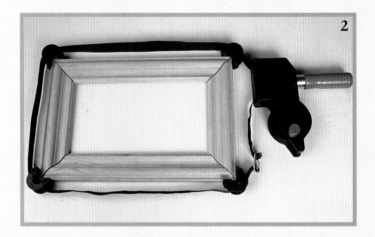

3. Apply a thin layer of wood glue to all surfaces to be joined. Avoid applying too much glue because it will squeeze out and make a mess.

4. Press glued joints together and position corner brackets.

5. Tighten strap clamp so that it is snug, but not tight. Measure frame to insure it is square, then tighten strap clamp and measure again.

6. Wipe off excess glue that may have been pushed out as joints were joined. Allow glue to completely dry, following manufacturer's instructions.

7. Remove strap clamp and corner brackets.

Nail joining

1. When fortifying the corners with nails, brads, or furniture staples clamp the joined frame flat onto work surface with the corner of joined frame extending past edge of the work surface.
   NOTE: Some framers only put nails in the top and bottom surface of the frame edges to keep nails from showing. Other framers use a cross pattern as shown on page 48 for greater strength.

2. Choose appropriate sized nails based on the size of the frame.

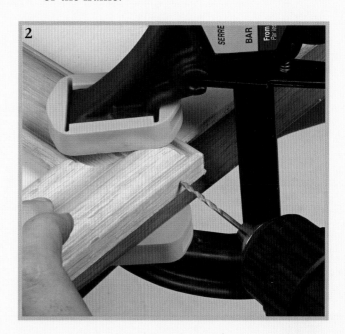

3. Drill one or two pilot holes per corner depending on size of molding. Make certain holes drilled are slightly smaller than nails to be used.

4. Hammer nails into place, then countersink them slightly beneath the surface of the frame.

5. Repeat nailing process on remaining three corners of the frame.

Staining and finishing the frame

1. Select your finish and fillers before beginning the project. Test on a small area of scrap material to make certain that finish color and sheen are correct. Test finish over filler that you are using to insure that they are compatible.

   NOTE: Many finishes can be applied to this type of frame. A stained finish was chosen for this project to give a basic understanding of the finishing process.

2. Lightly sand frame corners to make certain all glue, dirt, and oil are removed from surface of the frame.

3. Using fingers or tip of a flat screwdriver, fill all nail holes and gaps with wood filler.

4. Using utility knife remove all excess wood filler.

5. Allow wood filler to dry completely.

6. Sand filled areas lightly with (in the same direction as) the grain of the wood.

7. Refill any voids that remain (wood filler may shrink as it dries). Allow filler to dry, then sand again.

8. Apply stain, then varnish, following manufacturers' instructions. Since wood absorbs finishes at various rates, some areas may need a second or third coat of stain to properly blend or varnish to properly seal.

9. Insert frame package into frame and secure with finish nails.

Backing the frame

1. Apply a strip of double-sided tape $\frac{1}{16}$" from outside of frame on all sides.

2. Measure and cut kraft paper 2"–4" larger than frame. If necessary, splice two pieces of paper together to cover the entire back of the frame.

3. Roll up the length of the paper.

4. Adhere paper edge onto one side of the frame.

5. Carefully unroll paper over frame without allowing it to attach to the remaining sides. Pull the paper taut.

6. Adhere paper onto opposite side of frame.

7. Pull and adhere paper onto remaining sides.

8. Using utility knife, trim off excess paper.

Attaching the hanger

1. Choose D-strap hangers and braided wire heavy enough to hold framed picture on wall.

2. Measure height of the frame and divide by three. Measure and mark this calculated distance down from top of frame.

3. Examine profile of molding to decide what length of screw to use. The screw should never come within $\frac{1}{4}$" of the surface of the frame.

4. Drill small pilot holes, then screw D-strap hanger to the frame. The "D" part of the hangers should be pointing toward the center of frame.

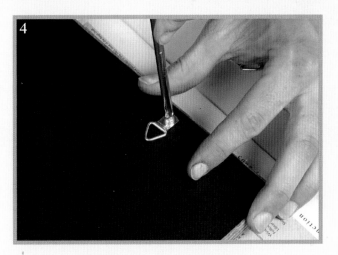

5. Tie braided wire to D-straps. Refer to page 38.

6. Place rubber or felt bumpers on bottom corners of frame.

4

Technique

Tools:
- 90° corner clamp
- Basic framing tools (see pages 10–11)
- Pneumatic brad gun

Materials:
- 1" Brads
- Double-sided tape
- Hanging system, D-strap and wire
- Kraft paper
- Offset clips
- Painting on stretched canvas
- Prefinished wood molding
- Rags or paper towels
- Rubber or felt bumpers
- Screws, size based on frame
- Translucent marker in matching color to the frame
- Wood filler in matching color to the frame, nonhardening
- Wood glue

How do I make a frame from prefinished wood molding?

Though more expensive, prefinished wood molding is just as easy to work as any other type of wood molding. The wide variety of colors and designs make custom framing truly worthwhile.

Framed Canvas

Activity concepts: Using a 90° corner clamp, joining with a brad gun, and using colored wood filler.

Here's how:

1. Determine size of frame. Refer to Measuring the molding on page 41.

2. Make certain to purchase enough molding. Refer to Molding Length Calculator on page 16.

3. Cut the molding. Refer to Cutting molding with a backsaw and a miter box on pages 41–42.

Gluing and joining the molding into a frame

A 90° corner clamp, as illustrated in this project, is fairly inexpensive and you really only need one to join a frame. I prefer to work with two, but one is just fine. These are available through any framing store or supplier.

1. Lay out frame pieces face up on a flat surface. Leave corners with a slight gap.

A prefinished matte black frame gives this painting a contemporary feel. Size: 20¾" x 24¾"

2. Apply a thin layer of wood glue to the surfaces of one mitered corner that will be joined. Press joint together and place it in 90° clamp immediately.

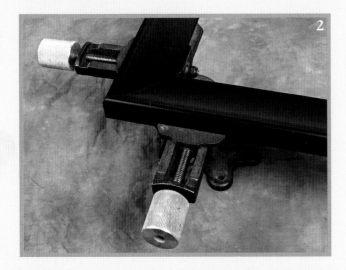

3. Wipe off excess glue on the frame.

Brad joining

1. While frame is in the 90° clamp, examine the profile of molding to determine placement of brads and ensure that length of brad is not going to pierce through front surface of frame. Select a spot and shoot brad.

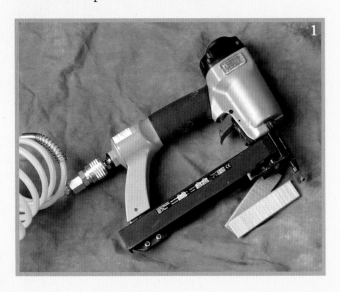

NOTES: Keep hands and fingers clear of frame, because brad could hit a hard spot or knot on the wood and veer into your finger.

Furniture staples may be substituted for brads. Pneumatic staple guns are used by professionals because they are fast and automatically countersink the brad or staple.

2. Stagger spacing and shoot one brad in each direction into frame. Frame corner is greatly stabilized with one brad going each way. If joining a larger frame, look for other areas on side of frame that could easily accommodate a brad.

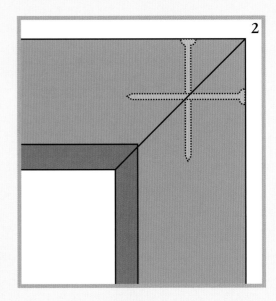

3. Remove joined corner from clamp. With brads in place, glue will dry without need of clamp.

4. If joining a large, thick frame, you may wish to invert joined corner and toenail more brads into back. Make certain that brads will not break through the front surface of frame.

5. Repeat Steps 2–7 for remaining corners.

Finishing a prefinished frame

1. Make certain that all glue is removed from surface of joined frame.

2. Burnish and round the corners with a screw driver shaft or an agate burnishing stone.

3. Use translucent markers to color seams and holes. Fill the holes with colored, nonhardening wood filler.

   NOTE: Mix colored nail-hole filler to match color of wood frame. For wood finishes that seem to have a great deal of depth, such as mahogany, add a little gold putty to simulate the luminous effect of the wood grain.

4. Wipe off excess wood filler with a soft cloth or paper towel.

   NOTE: This type of wood filler never becomes hard, so it is necessary to clean all filler from frame surface so it does not stain a carpet or anything else on which you may set frame.

Mounting a canvas in the frame

1. Set stretched canvas painting into frame rabbet. A portion of the canvas will probably protrude from frame.

2. Use offset clips to secure canvas. Drill pilot holes for screws.

   NOTE: Offset clamps come in various sizes can be purchased at frame shops or framing supply stores.

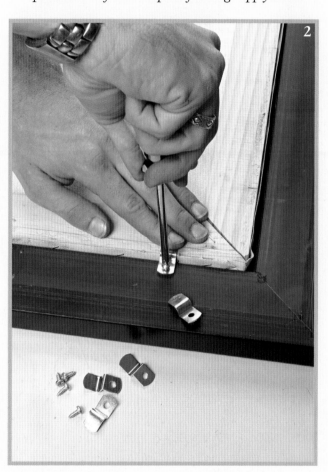

Finishing the frame

1. Back the frame with kraft paper. Refer to Backing the frame on page 45.

2. Attach a D-strap hanger and felt bumper pads. Refer to Attaching the hanger on page 45.

Technique

What you need to get started:

Tools:
- Basic framing tools (see pages 10–11)
- Ear plugs
- Forming tools
- Heat gun
- Point driver
- Power miter saw
- Safety Glasses
- Wood gouges

Materials:
- Antiquing dust
- Cardboard, cut to fit mirror
- Mirror
- Nails, brads, or staples
- Ornate molding of your choice
- Sandpaper, 200-grit
- Translucent marker in matching color to the frame
- Wood filler in matching color to the frame, nonhardening
- Wood glue

How do I make a frame from ornate molding?

Ornate molding is made into a frame exactly like any other type of prefinished molding. However, greater care must be taken so the pattern or texture of the frame does not become distracting where the mitered corners meet.

Ornate Mirror

Activity concepts: Cutting molding with a power miter saw, matching ornate pattern at the corners, blending frame patterns, touching up pattern adjustment, framing mirror.

Here's how:

1. Determine size of frame. Refer to Measuring the molding on page 41.

2. Make certain to purchase enough molding. Refer to Molding Length Calculator on page 16.

Cutting molding with a power miter saw

NOTE: Safety first. Be certain to wear safety glasses and ear plugs while using a power miter saw. The ear plugs will keep you from becoming distracted by the noise of the saw. Additionally, some power saws are loud enough to cause temporary or permanent hearing loss. Operate equipment as per manufacturer's instruction and with all safety items in place and in good condition. Do not wear long-sleeved shirts or hand and wrist jewelry. Use clamps on the molding to keep your fingers away from the blades.

Ornate frames work well with hand-beveled mirrors because the frame makes the mirror a prominent feature in whatever location it is placed. Size: 23½" x 30"

1. Place molding on bed of the saw with rabbet facing you and the molding stock to left of saw. If molding is too long it may need to be supported .

2. Align back edge of molding with saw blade at a 45° angle to the left.

3. Clamp molding into place. The clamp holds molding securely while cutting, providing a cleaner, more accurate cut.

4. Once everything is ready, release safety mechanism(s) and start blade while in the upright position. Starting blade while partially lowered may jerk saw and damage molding.

5. After allowing blade to reach its maximum speed, slowly lower blade as it cuts through molding. Push handle all the way down and hold it there for a moment to assure cut is totally finished.

6. Allow blade to stop moving before raising handle. This will prevent a second, less accurate cut from being made. This also prevents saw blade from grabbing the scrap piece and flinging it in an unexpected direction.

7. Measure back edge of frame from the mitered end to the longest "C" dimension determined. Mark off and cut a long side of framing. By cutting a longer sides first, you allow for possible mistakes. If you make a mistake, you can cut the molding down to make a smaller side.

8. Change miter saw to a 45° angle to the right.

9. Align blade with the mark, then clamp molding firmly on both sides of blade. Keep in mind waste side of blade, so that you do not cut off too much.

10. Repeat Steps 4–6 on page 52.

11. Repeat Steps 1–10 for second long side.

12. Repeat Steps 1–10 for both short sides.

13. To insure that opposite frame pieces are the exact length, place them back to back. If they are not exactly the same, trim a little off longer one until they are exactly the same length.

Matching ornate corner patterns

It is not necessary to match corner patterns exactly due to a great deal of inconsistency in these patterns making it nearly impossible to get a perfect match. Additionally, when closely matched, corners seem to distract from the artwork. Treat ornamentation as texture rather than pattern.

1. Cut the first length of molding as you would any other molding.

2. Match mitered corners as best as you can so there is the least amount of difference in relief.

NOTE: Some geometric moldings require more planning during cutting so patterns match up adequately. Work from one corner to the next. Slice off small sections from first cut of each successive side until pattern match is satisfactory. Last section is hardest because it must blend with two other corners.

3. Join corners with glue. Refer to Gluing and joining the molding into a frame on pages 42–43 or pages 46–48.

4. Join the corners with nails. Refer to Nail joining on page 43, or Brad joining on page 48.

Blending the molding texture

To blend molding texture, you will need to know what type of material the ornamentation is composed of. Ornamentation is usually made of four general types of material.

Particleboard. Typically this is a wood sawdust product, mixed with glues and molded into ornamentation, then applied to the surface after being steamed. These can be:

- Carved so the pattern matches better .

Carving to match pattern

- Sanded, then refinished with marker, nail hole filler, antiquing dust, or guilder's cream.

Plaster or acrylic-based gesso. This material is typically white in color and is formed directly onto the surface of molding. Be careful with plaster, it can be easily broken. Gesso is much more resilient. This can be:

• Carved to match the pattern, then sanded smooth. Follow the same tooling and finishing tips as for composition material.

Heat-activated resin products. This molding is made in large sections and machine applied using heat-activated adhesives. These can be:

• Remolded by using a heat gun on low or hair dryer on high.

1. Warm the surface until it becomes pliable and use whatever tools are available with different shaped tips to obtain the desired pattern.

2. Hold molding in place until it cools and becomes hard. Carefully work on only one corner at a time.

3. Touch up surface with a matching marker, colored wood filler, antiquing dust, or guilder's cream.

Heat-embossed wooden molding. Using a heated brass wheel, wooden molding is passed through embosser under great pressure, which creates a pattern in the wood itself. Typically this type of frame needs little finish work because ornamentation has shallow relief. This can be:

• Touched up with a marker and colored wood filler. Pay special attention to the front surface.

• Burnished with a burnishing tool or a screwdriver shaft on raised ornamentation to make pattern blend better.

Frame finishing

1. Insert mirror and cardboard backing into frame.

2. Mirror may be secured with nails, but a point driver is a much better tool for this application. It is easy to break the glass when hammering in nails.

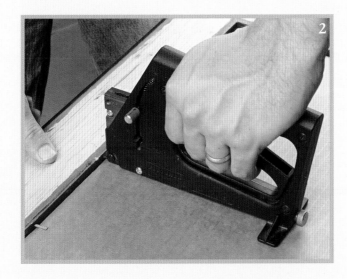

An ornamental frame can make the most ordinary picture seem like it is a priceless treasure.

3. Back the frame with kraft paper. Refer to Backing the frame on page 45.

4. Attach a D-strap hanger mounted vertically on each side of the frame about ⅓ the way down from top. Hanging mirror directly from D-straps allows mirror to hang closer to wall without tipping out.
NOTE: The location of the D-straps must be carefully measured or mirror will hang crookedly.

5. Install felt or rubber bumpers on bottom corners. Refer to Attaching the hanger Step 6 on page 45.

The elegance of an ornamental frame not only affects the picture it surrounds, but the entire room.

How do I make a barn–wood frame?

Barn-wood frames have a great deal of character and are widely used. Methods of joinery can become very ingenious with these frames, utilizing horse tackle, farm implement parts, leather, and rusty nails or bolts. Use these basic instructions and expand on them to come up with something of your own.

Framed Farm Implement

Activity concepts: Selecting and preparing barn wood, cutting into shape, painting raw wood, applying protective sealant, making shadow box.

Here's how:

1. Choose wood that is structurally strong.

2. Inspect the wood to make certain all nails and other pieces of material that may damage saw blades have been removed.

3. Rip wood on a table saw to the correct dimensions for the intended project.
   NOTE: Allow ⅜″ more depth than item to be set in shadow box.

This rusty piece of farm machinery looks wonderful displayed in a shadowbox framed with barn wood. Size: 12" x 12½"

4. Using the table saw with a dado blade or a router with a rabbet bit, cut a deep rabbet into one edge of frame material.

5. Build the frame. Refer to Techniques 3 and 4 on pages 39–49.

6. Sand all visible edges of frame with the grain of the wood until there are deep gouges in the wood. A wire wheel or brush can also be used.

7. Mix brown and black acrylic paints, then thin with water until color and intensity match the color of barn wood. Brush onto unfinished edges. Allow paint to dry, then reapply if necessary.

8. Use a clear matte spray finish to seal the wood and eliminate barn odors.

NOTE: An oil-based finish, will bring out much more color in most barn-wood frames. This can be desirable or undesirable depending on the item you choose to place in the shadow box).

Assembling the shadow box

1. Cut mat backing to size of rabbet opening plus depth of shadow box.

2. Draw four lines on back of mat based on depth determined for shadow box.

3. Using craft knife, score lines and cut out corners.

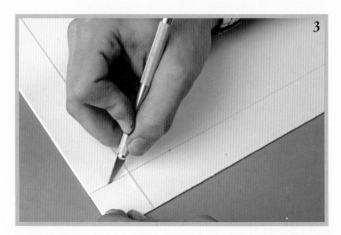

4. Fold mat into box shape.

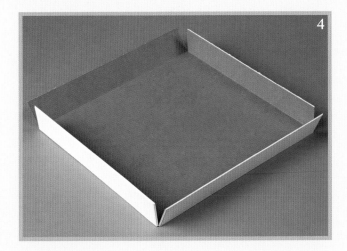

5. Tape corners together.

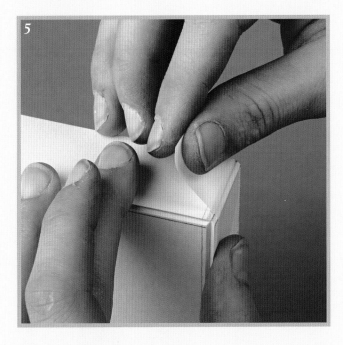

6. Hot-glue the farm implement into place in shadow box .
NOTES: *When mounting heavier items, it is a good idea to use a piece of ¼" plywood behind the backing for support.*

Glue will hold better if a hole is drilled in the mat board so it can flow through and adhere to back side of mat board.

7. Attach frames and other wooden nonvaluable items to backing with screws.
NOTE: *Some items such as spoons, guns, and records have premade mounting systems that you can purchase at a frame shop.*

8. Insert shadow-box frame package into frame and secure with glue, nails, or offset clamps.

Frame finishing

1. Back the frame with kraft paper. Refer to Backing the frame on page 45.

2. If frame is small and lightweight, attach a sawtooth hanger. Refer to Attaching a sawtooth hanger on page 30. If frame is heavy, attach a D-strap and wire hanger. Refer to Attaching the hanger on page 45.

A barn-wood frame with a twist is this basic barn-wood frame with matching colored decorative molding layered on top.

How do I cut a beveled mat for my picture?

After properly measuring and laying out the location to cut, the mat-cutter blade can easily cut a window with beveled edges.

Framed Quilt Block

Activity concepts: Determining mat style, selecting measuring style, cutting beveled mat, mounting quilt block.

Here's how:

1. Select an appropriate mat. Refer to Selecting an Appropriate Mat on pages 24–25.

Determine proper mat style

There are various mat styles. The one you choose should match the style of artwork and the decor of the room where the picture will be displayed.

Standard mat. This simple style has equal mat margins on all four sides of the mat. Because the standard mat is not visually weighted, many people will comment that a standard mat looks poorly proportioned.

Standard mat

An heirloom quilt block made from a daughter's childhood dresses is softly enhanced by an ornate frame and a simple beveled mat. Size: 17½" x 17½"

Visually weighted mat. This is the most natural looking mat. The top and sides are equal width with a slightly wider bottom. A good way to calculate how much larger the bottom should be is to multiply the width on the top or side margin by 1.16 then round up to the nearest ⅛". For example, on a mat that has a 3" top margin, the bottom should be 3½". Most people will not notice that the bottom is wider than the top or the sides.

Heavily weighted mat. This mat style is best used when decorating in a modern or more contemporary environment. The top and sides are equal, and often oversized. The bottom is heavily weighted at approximately 1.5–2 times the width of the top and side margins. This style is most appropriate for abstract, nonrealistic types of artwork, or sketches.

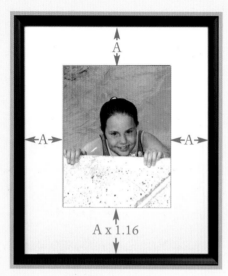

Visually weighted mat

Heavily weighted mat

Vertically enhancing mat. This mat style is best used when you have a piece that is vertical in shape or has an overall vertical "feel." The sides are equal and the top is 1.33 times the width of the sides. The bottom is 1.5 times the width of the sides. This style works great on vertical scrolls and tall, slender paintings. Using a standard mat with a tall piece will ruin the vertical feel of the picture. The larger the mat margins, the less "skinny" the artwork will feel.

Vertically enhancing mat

Collection mats. When framing for an exhibit or other type of groupings, it is sometimes desirable to have all of the frames the same size. This gives a real sense of consistency to the artwork, even though the individual pieces may be of different shapes and sizes. The best way to do this is to group all of the artwork to be framed. Take the width measurement from the widest picture and the height measurement from the tallest picture. Add 3" to all four sides. This will be the size of your mat blocks, glass, backing and inside frame dimensions. Then position each picture to fit slightly high in the mat.

Collection mat

Determine mat window style

Standard mat. Measure the exact size of the artwork. Subtract ¼" from each dimension to provide a little overlap room. Add on the desired mat margins.

Photo or print mat. These are commonly used throughout the professional photography and print fields. Artists using these mediums traditionally sign and title their work close under the image on the white unprinted paper. This style is also used on signed and numbered posters when the artist has chosen to sign in the white space rather than on the reproduction itself.

Calculate the exact size of the image and add ¼" to the top and sides and ⅜" to the bottom to allow for title and signature. Sometimes extra white space must be added to the bottom for more flamboyant signatures. After calculating the image plus white space, add on the desired mat margins. Typically a visually weighted mat is the best choice here.

NOTE: In the example below, a colored frame was chosen rather than one of black or silver. This is done to help sell the print when a formal display frame is not required.

Photo or print mat

63

Float mat. This mat style is appropriate when the entire image must show and the image goes to the edge of the paper, or as with contemporary watercolors on paper with a finished edge or art with a deckled or decorative edge. The mat is cut the same as a photo or print mat, with the exception that the "white space" between the mat and the artwork is actually the backing material. The artwork is thus "floating" inside the mat.

Cutting a beveled mat window

1. Measure picture to determine overall mat size and the eventual size of the "window" in the center of mat.

2. Place a clean slip sheet over work table.
   NOTE: A slip sheet is a smooth sheet of fiberboard or scrap mat board. Its purpose is to protect the work table, keep the mat cutter blade sharp, and allow the mat-cutter to make clean straight cuts. Care must be taken so new cuts do not intersect previously made cut lines on the slip sheet. Cut lines can pull the mat cutter blade off course and result in a crooked cut.

3. Place mat board face down on slip sheet.

4. Using a hard-lead pencil and a T-square, mark off the outside dimensions of the mat. Extend lines ⅛" past each inside corner and make a mark to show where to stop cutting.

5. With a straight mat cutter, cut out mat block.

6. Remove excess mat board from work table and with mat face down, carefully mark out center hole using hard-lead pencil and T-square. Once again, extend lines ⅛" past corners to mark stopping point of the cut.
   NOTE: Most hand-held mat cutters have a small mark to show where to start and stop the cuts.

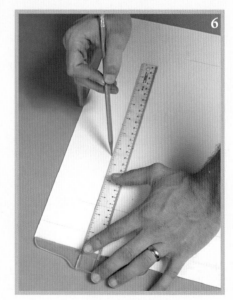

7. Carefully position mat over slip sheet for first cut.

8. Position the mat-cutter blade over the line on back of mat. Before cutting, check to make certain the bevel of the cut is going the correct direction toward front of mat.

9. Insert blade into mat and cut with smooth even pressure on both mat-cutter head and mat guide for full length of the cut. The key to a good cut is a smooth even motion.

10. Retract the blade and repeat Steps 7–9 on the remaining three sides.

Fitting quilt block into mat

1. Cut a piece of backing to same size as mat.

2. Apply framing tape to top of quilt block with sticky side up.

3. Set quilt block on table and lower mat into position. Press mat down so tape will stick to it.

4. Turn mat and quilt block over. Stretch quilt block by taping each edge of the quilt block onto mat.

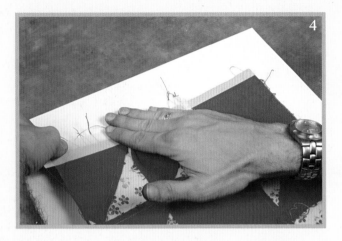

5. Check the front of quilt block frequently to assure it is being stretched and secured properly.

Frame finishing

1. Fit frame package (mat, quilt block, and backing) into selected frame and secure. Refer to Frame finishing on page 30.

2. Back the frame with kraft paper. Refer to Backing the frame on page 45.

3. Attach a sawtooth hanger. Refer to Attaching a sawtooth hanger on page 30.

A colored core mat can almost appear as a double mat. In this case, a multiple mat would overpower the picture while the single mat keeps the dark oversized frame in perfect balance.

A small print can be framed in an oversized mat and frame. This picture would not have the same impact if it was displayed in a smaller frame.

How do I make a multiple beveled mat for my picture?

If you can cut a single beveled mat, simply adjust the measurements and cut another mat with a different sized window.

Multiple-matted Photograph

Activity concepts: Cutting multiple mats, hinging with nonarchival tape.

Here's how:

1. Select an appropriate mat. Refer to Selecting an Appropriate Mat on pages 24–25.

2. Determine proper mat style and mat window style. Refer to Determine proper mat style and Determine mat window style on pages 60–64.

Cutting multiple beveled mat windows

1. Select the number and color of mats to use. For this project we will use three mats.

2. Determine how much of the center and bottom mat will be showing. For this project, we have chosen to show ⅛" on all sides for the center mat and ¼" for the bottom mat.

3. Determine overall mat size (mat block) and measure photo to identify needed size of "window" for mat closest to picture, or bottom mat.

What you need to get started:

Tools:
• Basic framing tools (see pages 10–11)

Materials:
• Double-sided tape
• Foam-core backing
• Frame, ready-made or custom built
• Framing tape
• Hanging hardware
• Kraft paper
• Mat boards (3)
• Photograph, 4" x 6"
• Slip sheet

An ordinary snapshot of Trafalgar Square is enhanced by a triple mat and tastefully weighty frame. Size: 15" x 13"

4. Place a clean slip sheet on work table. With straight mat cutter, cut top mat to fit into frame. Cut other two mat blocks ¼" smaller in both width and height. This will allow you to line up reveal in mat windows without the outside edges interfering.

5. Place top mat onto slip sheet and plot out window opening, making all measurements ⅜" larger on all sides.
NOTE: Center mat window will measure ¼" larger on all sides.

6. Cut out beveled window from front mat. Refer to Cutting a beveled mat window on pages 64–65. Make certain center scrap piece is completely cut out and can fall free.

7. Replace center piece back into front mat and place double-sided tape in the middle of the scrap piece. Also place double-sided tape around back sides of top mat. Center the center mat on top of front, or top, mat and stick center mat in

place on top mat. This allows scrap piece to act as a fresh slip sheet for the second series of cuts. It also fixes center mat onto top mat.

8. Plot out location for center mat window by measuring from the edges of top mat. Repeat Steps 6 and 7.

9. Place bottom mat onto mat pile and secure with double-sided tape to both the scrap piece of center mat and outside edges of the center mat. Repeat measuring and cutting processes. The resulting mats should have the front mat with the largest window. The center mat should have a ⅛" reveal and the bottom mat will have a ¼" reveal. The mats will also be attached together properly.

Nonarchival tape hinge

1. Using a straight mat cutter, cut a piece of archival foam-core backing to fit into the selected frame and matching the size of top mat.

2. Apply two strips of framing tape horizontally to reverse side of photograph. Make certain only ¼" of tape is attached to photograph. Apply tape to the top of the photograph. Taping other edges will cause photograph to warp.

3. Lay mat stack over the photograph and center the image in mat window.

4. Apply pressure to front of mat over the taped area so tape will stick.

5. Invert mat and rub tape from the back to insure proper adhesion.

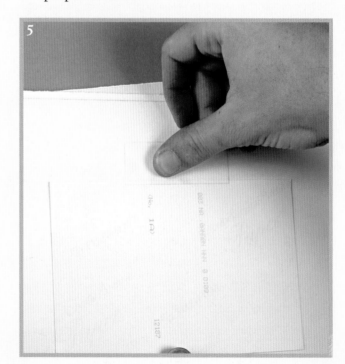

Frame finishing

1. Fit frame package (mat stack, photograph, and backing) into selected frame and secure. Refer to Frame finishing on page 30.

2. Back the frame with kraft paper. Refer to Backing the frame on page 45.

3. Attach a sawtooth hanger. Refer to Attaching a sawtooth hanger on page 30.

Multiple mats do not have to be different colors. Sometimes they work to give depth and character to a picture.

Mat cut-outs are very popular for several types of artwork. Multiple mats provide more possibilities for this technique.

9
Technique

What you need to get started:

Tools:
- Basic framing tools (see pages 10–11)

Materials:
- Archival foam-core backing
- Double-sided tape
- Fabric hinging tape
- Frame, ready-made or custom built
- Framing tape
- Gummed Japanese rice paper
- Hanging hardware
- Kraft paper
- Mat board
- Paintings

How do I make an archival mount?

There are two general types of archival mounts. The focus of these mounts is to avoid any possible damage to the paper or the artwork when framing or displaying the piece.

Archival Artwork

Activity concepts: Mounting T-hinges, mounting V-hinges, using fabric hinging tape, using gummed Japanese rice paper.

Here's how:

1. Select an appropriate mat. Refer to Selecting an Appropriate Mat on pages 24–25.

2. Determine proper mat style and mat window style. Refer to Determine proper mat style and Determine mat window style on pages 60–64.

3. Cut an archival foam-core backing to match size of the mat.

T-hinge mount

For archival mounting, I use high-quality tape; however, when framing something on thin paper, use Japanese rice-paper hinges.

1. Hinge the cut mat onto the archival backing, using fabric hinging tape.

Archival quality materials and mounting techniques insure this watercolor will last many lifetimes. Size: 22¼" x 18¾"

2. Center artwork onto backing, using the mat window as a guide.

3. Adhere two 1" lengths of framing tape vertically onto top and back of artwork. Only ¼" of the tape should be adhered onto artwork. Any more could cause warping of the paper.

4. Adhere a 2" piece of framing tape horizontally over vertical pieces of tape, adhering them onto the backing.

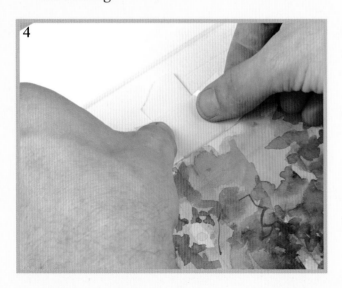

5. Fold mat back into place.

6. Fit frame package into selected frame and secure. Refer to Frame finishing on page 30.

7. Back the frame with kraft paper. Refer to Backing the frame on page 45.
   NOTE: Archival mounts are designed to minimize damage to the artwork.

V-hinge mount

This is used when doing a float mount. The hinge does not show from the front so it allows edge of the artwork to be seen.

1. Just as with T-mount, hinge the cut mat onto archival backing, using fabric hinging tape (see page 72).

2. Position artwork onto backing, using mat window as a guide and hold in place.

3. Using hard-lead pencil, make very light marks on backing at top of the artwork. Mark the top and sides.

4. Flip artwork vertically and position in relationship with index lines that you drew.

5. Adhere two 1" pieces of framing tape, adhering them onto top of artwork and extending about the same distance onto backing.

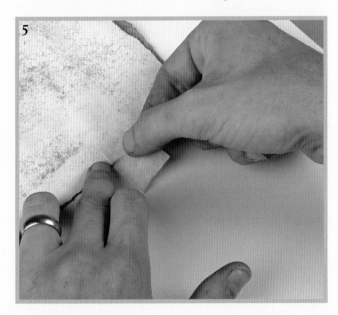

6. Apply another two pieces of framing tape horizontally so that top of the tape just touches edge of artwork.

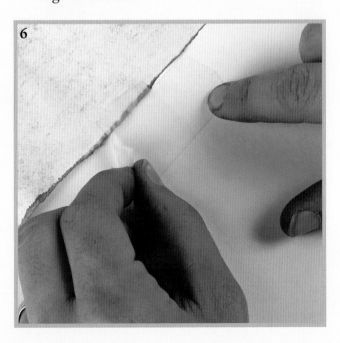

7. Fold the artwork into place on backing.

8. Fold mat back into place.

9. Fit frame package into selected frame and secure. Refer to Frame finishing on page 30.

10. Back the frame with kraft paper. Refer to Backing the frame on page 45.
NOTE: When float-mounting, you can use a colored mat for backing to give an accent to the recessed background area.

Section 3: Projects

1
Project

What you need to get started:

Tools:
- Basic framing tools (see pages 10–11)

Materials:
- Archival foam-core backing
- Double-sided tape
- Double-sided stitchery tape
- Frame, ready-made or custom built
- Framing tape
- Glass (optional)
- Hanging hardware
- Kraft paper
- Mat board(s)
- Stitchery item

How do I frame a cross–stitched piece?

Framed fabric items must have an adjustable mount. This project shows how it is done.

Framed Cross-stitch

Activity concepts: Mounting fabric using stitchery tape, controlling humidity.

Here's how:

1. Select a frame and mat combination based on the artwork. Refer to Selecting an Appropriate Mat on pages 24–25.

2. Cut mats. Refer to Cutting multiple beveled mat windows on pages 67–69.

3. Cut backing to the same size as mats.

4. Cut out window from backing that is ¼" larger all around the mat window. Place cut-out piece on work surface.

The right frame turns a cross-stitched piece into a treasured heirloom. Size: 11" x 22¼"

5   Adhere double-sided stitchery tape around edge of cutout; this will be the back side.

NOTES: *This stitchery tape is archival and will not yellow or permanently bond. Most self-adhesive foam-core backings made for stitchery will cause damage to the cross-stitch in a few years. Additionally, adhering the stitchery to the face of the adhesive does not allow for a perfect mounting. Furthermore, dust will be attracted to the adhesive and collect on the face of the cross-stitch.*

I use the tape method rather than pins because I feel that it allows for a more even contraction of the fabric over time. Pins can create a scalloped pattern in the cloth if the cloth shrinks. Should you choose to use pins, use only blunt-tipped stainless steel pins pressed into the outside edge of the backing.

6. Mount backing with window cutout onto back of the mat with double-sided or ATG tape.

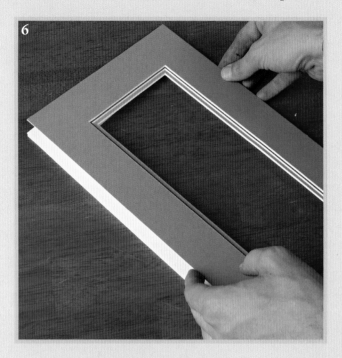

7. Center cross-stitch in window.

8. Press the cutout into the window. This may take a few tries to get the stitchery centered properly in the middle.

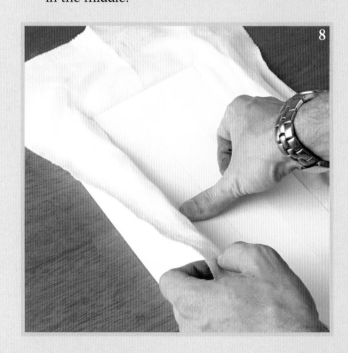

9. Choose the corner that looks the closest to how you want the finished piece to look. Start pulling fabric through backing and adhere it onto stitchery tape on the back. Work from the first corner all the way around. You may have to readjust fabric slightly by pulling on certain parts a second or even a third time around.

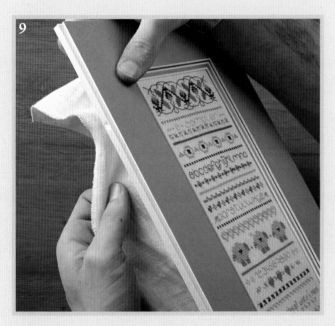

10. Invert the stretched piece and tape backing into window with framing tape.

11. Cut a sheet of scrap mat to fit over the back.

Frame finishing

1. Fit frame package into selected frame and secure. Refer to Frame finishing on page 30.

2. Back the frame with kraft paper. Refer to Backing the frame on page 45.

3. Attach a sawtooth hanger. Refer to Attaching a sawtooth hanger on page 30.

Glass or no glass

This decision depends on your climate and the location in your house where you plan to display the framed stitchery. In climates that are quite dry, it is usually recommend to use glass. Dust accumulation on an unglazed piece can affect the fabric.

If placing the stitchery into a kitchen or bathroom, it is best to glaze it and seal it tightly. The high relative humidity in these areas can cause severe damage to the fabric. If the frame package is not properly sealed, then it allows moisture to condense on the glass and create mildew and mold problems.

If you are in a humid climate and never get a dry day (relative humidity of less than 20%) it will be very difficult to make a sealed frame package that will not have moisture problems. Professional framers build humidity controlled rooms for this purpose. If you live in such a climate, take your stitchery to a professional to seal or leave the item unglazed. Avoid placing an unglazed framed piece in a kitchen because of the air-borne grease and oils.

2
Project

What you need to get started:

Tools:
- Basic framing tools (see pages 10–11)
- Hot-glue gun

Materials:
- Double-sided tape
- Foam-core backing
- Frame, ready-made or custom built
- Framing tape
- Glass
- Hanging hardware
- Hot-glue sticks
- Kraft paper
- Mat boards (2)
- Multiple pictures

How do I make a multiple–opening mat?

To make a mat with multiple openings only requires more measuring and a few more cuts.

Multiple-opening Mat

Activity concepts: Measuring for multiple mat windows.

Here's how:

1. Lay items to be framed out in a pleasing arrangement. It is not necessary to create a symmetrical layout for the composition of images to be balanced; however, it is important to get the spaces between items balanced.

Some items need to be in a grouping. Together, they say more than they could individually.
A multiple-opening mat is perfect for this type of display. Size: 13¼" x 18½"

2. Determine overall size of mat to be framed.

3. Cut top mat and bottom mat to same size.

4. Cut backing and glass to match mat block size. Refer to Cutting glass on pages 34–36. You now have a frame package blank.

5. Select a ready-made frame or build frame. Refer to Techniques 3 and 4 on pages 39–49.

6. Go back to your picture arrangement. Measure each item that you want to use in the collage and using a T-square, draw out the design on back of top mat, adding mat reveal to the dimensions. You must also subtract a little for mat overlap on each photo.

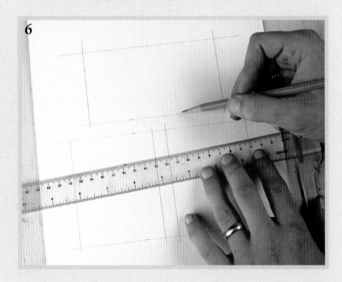

7. Cut out each mat window. Refer to Cutting a beveled mat window on pages 64–65.

8. Invert and stack both mats, with bottom mat on bottom of stack.

9. Trace cut-out windows onto back of bottom mat, then measure the reveal for each window; or attach a piece of mat board or foam-core to the pencil with tape.
    NOTE: The thicker the material, the wider the reveal.

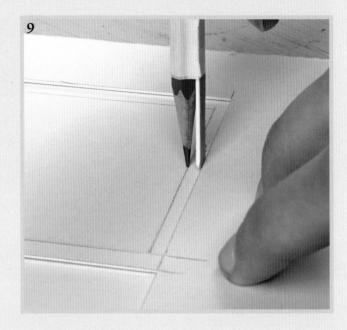

10. Cut out the bottom mat windows.

11. Adhere mats together with double-sided or ATG tape.

12. Hinge photos onto back mat with framing tape tape. Refer to Nonarchival tape hinge on page 70.

13. Hot-glue other items onto backing.

Frame finishing

1. Fit frame package into selected frame and secure. Refer to Frame finishing on page 30.

2. Back the frame with kraft paper. Refer to Backing the frame on page 45.

3. Attach a sawtooth hanger. Refer to Attaching a sawtooth hanger on page 30.

How do I tint a gold frame?

Tinting a frame is easy and it can give a frame that perfect touch. The trick is to choose the right color and tint the frame slowly until the perfect color is achieved.

Gold Tinted Frame

Activity concepts: Selecting tints, mixing tints, tinting a frame, antiquing a frame.

Many people use ready-mades to frame their work. In most cases, a custom frame would look better; however, money or time constraints can make it difficult to find something that works well with the artwork. Many ready-made frames are a bright gold color. There are many things that can be done to tint the frame to a more suitable hue without losing the nice "leaved" look of the frame. Keep in mind, this method does not work for every picture. However, it is durable, fast, easy, and requires little practice.

Here's how:

1. Choose a frame that is the proper size and style for the size of artwork you have. Refer to Selecting a frame pages 20–23.

2. Decide what color you would like the frame to be tinted. For an overall, cooler, more subtle finish, I use a white. To bring out some of the greens in the trees, I use a blue-green transparent glaze over the gold.
   NOTE: A good way to select an appropriate color for a picture is to go to a paint store and choose paint chips like you would choose a mat color for a picture.

3. Have person mixing the paint mix chosen color into a clear acrylic or polyurethane finish rather than a paint body. You

What you need to get started:

Tools:
- Basic framing tools (see pages 10–11)

Materials:
- Automotive parts-cleaning brush
- Gold frame, ready-made
- Hanging hardware
- Kraft paper
- Picture
- Rottenstone
- Sandpaper, 400-grit
- Soft, lint-free rags
- Spray adhesive
- Tint in polyurethane finish

*The perfect shade of gold for a frame is no accident. Tinting and antiquing can make
the perfect frame both for your artwork and for the room in which it will be displayed. Size: 21" x 25"*

choose the sheen based on the final finish you desire. As a general rule, a semigloss is usually best. If you want a smooth thick finish, you might consider an oil-based finish. Most people prefer faster-drying finishes applied in multiple thin layers.

Applying the tint

1. Lightly sand frame with 400-grit sandpaper.

2. Clean all dust and debris from frame and work surface with a rag.

3. With frame lying face up on work table, dip the tip of a clean dry rag in chosen finish and rub generously onto frame. Because you must work quickly, the process may become messy.

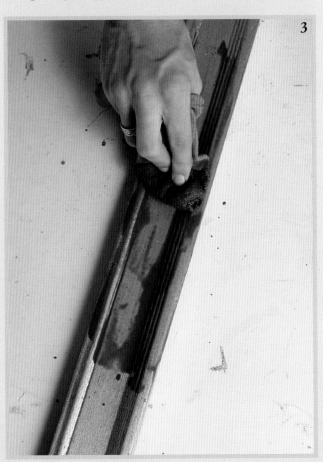

4. With another clean dry rag, immediately wipe all excess finish from frame. Take care not to leave draglines at the corners. You will not notice much of a difference with first coat. These finishes are designed to be very smooth and subtle.

5. Allow finish to become dry to the touch.

6. Apply additional coats. Continue this process until frame reaches desired color. Check it periodically against the artwork as frame color may change more than is visibly apparent while you are working on it.

Antiquing with rottenstone

Rottenstone, or antiquing dust, is ground-up stone made into a fine powder. There are many different varieties and colors. This method of application is very simple, but as it is a powdery dust, it might be best to do it outdoors.

1. Spray ornamented areas of frame with spray adhesive. Apply additional adhesive to corner areas. Do not allow adhesive to puddle deeply.

2. Allow to dry from 30 seconds to one minute or until tacky but not wet.

3. Apply rottenstone liberally with an automotive parts-cleaning brush.

4. Wipe immediately with a rag to remove dust from the high spots.

5. Allow to fully dry according to the instructions on the adhesive.

NOTE: Many professional frame restorers will apply the rottenstone with the frame hung rather than flat. This gives a more realistic "dust" build up; however, the finish is less even.

Frame finishing

1. Fit frame package into selected frame and secure. Refer to Frame finishing on page 30.

2. Back the frame with kraft paper. Refer to Backing the frame on page 45.

3. Attach a D-strap hanger and felt bumper pads. Refer to Attaching the hanger on pages 45.

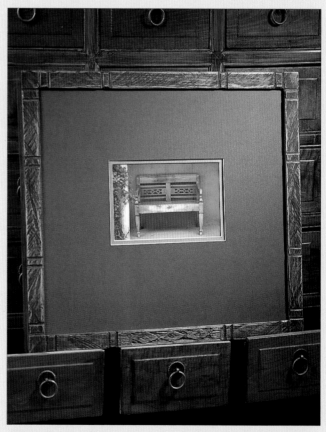

There are many ways to tint and antique a frame. This particular handmade frame was stained, distressed, and painted to get that perfect aged appearance.

How do I frame a print for a museum display?

Simple but sturdy components and archival quality materials are hallmarks of museum displays.

Framed Museum Display

Activity concepts: Using archival tape and backing, using conservation corners.

Most museums and galleries require that photos and prints be printed with a minimum of 1"–1½" of white space around the image. This is to ensure that any damage to the piece while being handled will not be viewed when the mat is in place. True photography and print mediums are to be treated as original artwork and are not reproducible. In the darkroom or print studio, they are tediously perfected and should be framed to enhance that perfection. When choosing a mat color, match the color of the paper edge around the image.

Here's how:

1. Refer to Determine proper mat style and Determine mat window style on pages 60–64. Pay special attention to Photo or print mat on page 63.

2. Cut mat and backing. Refer to Cutting a beveled mat window on pages 64–65.

3. Hinge the cut mat onto backing with fabric hinging tape. Refer to T-hinge mount on pages 72–74.

What you need to get started:

Tools:
• Basic framing tools (see pages 10–11)

Materials:
• Archival fabric hinging tape
• Archival foam-core backing
• Conservation corners
• Display frame
• Double-sided tape
• Frame, ready-made or custom built
• Glass
• Kraft paper
• Photograph or print
• Mat board
• Hanging hardware

When framing photographs or prints for professional competition or display, certain rules must be followed. It is important to know these rules so that the artwork is displayed in the best possible condition. Size: 11" x 14"

4. Center image in mat window.

5. Use conservation corners to attach photograph or print to backing.

6. Close the hinged mat.

7. Cut the glass. Refer to Cutting glass on pages 34–36.

Finishing the frame

1. Fit frame package into selected frame and secure. Refer to Frame finishing on page 30.

2. Back the frame with kraft paper. Refer to Backing the frame on page 45.

3. Attach a D-strap hanger and felt bumper pads. Refer to Attaching the hanger on pages 45.
   NOTES: *These mediums are well presented in a simple black frame. Extruded aluminum frames work very well and can be purchased as sectionals or made by a frame shop. The ready-made metal frames are typically too thin and flimsy looking to add any credibility to the artwork.*

I use a matte-black wooden frame that has a very refined surface and finishes well. Look at a frame sample and notice how easily it scratches and shows fingerprints. Some of the less expensive ones actually last very well while others mar easily.

5
Project

What you need to get started:

Tools:
- Basic framing tools (see pages. 10–11)
- Fabric scissors

Materials:
- Fabric of your choice
- Mat board
- Newspaper
- Spray adhesive
- Slip sheet

How do I make a fabric-covered mat?

Spray adhesive makes it easy to adhere fabric onto a precut mat.

Fabric-covered Mat

Activity concepts: Adhering fabric onto a mat.

Fabric-covered mats provide a great deal of flexibility. You can add texture and intense color not available in traditional mats.

Here's how:

1. Cut a mat complete with window. Refer to Technique 7 on pages 60–66. Any color mat works with opaque fabrics, but white or off-white mats work best for fabrics that allow the mat to show through.

2. Choose a fabric. You can use many of the same principles and guidelines used for choosing a mat and frame. Refer to Selecting an Appropriate Mat on pages 24–25.

3. Cut fabric 2" larger all around than mat.

4. Place fabric face down and mat face up on a flat newspaper. *NOTE: The fabric must be very smooth. Wrinkles will be very hard, if not impossible, to remove.*

5. Spray both surfaces liberally.

6. Allow fabric and mat to dry for one minute.

Sometimes the perfect mat cannot be found, but it can be made by covering a white mat with a carefully selected piece of material. Size: 9¾" x 11¾"

7. Adhere mat onto fabric.

8. Place fabric and mat face down on a slip sheet and cut a window in fabric 1"–2" smaller all around the mat window.

9. Make a slit that starts ⅛" from inside corner of mat window and extends at 45° angle to center window of the fabric.

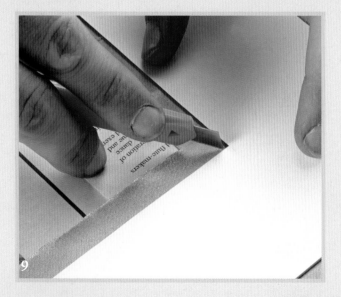

10. Spray back of mat and fabric tabs with spray adhesive.

11. Allow adhesive to dry for one minute. Then carefully attach tabs in frame window to the back of mat. Trim fabric to edge of mat with a sharp craft knife.

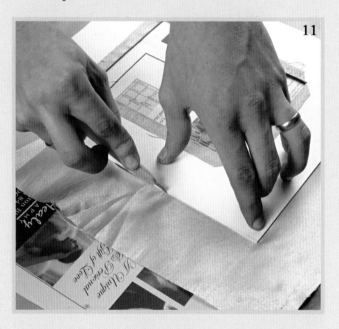

12. Allow fabric to completely dry and adhere tightly onto mat.

13. Use as a normal mat.

How do I mount and frame coins to see both sides?

All it takes is a little extra cutting and you can see both sides of a mounted coin.

Mounted Coins

Activity concepts: Mounting within mat board, cutting circles, double-sided glazing.

Most coins and medallions have two unique sides. It is a shame to only see one side. I have created a mounting style that is easy and allows the framed coin to be viewed from either side.

Here's how:

1. Cut two pieces of mat board the size of the frame. Refer to Cutting a beveled mat window on pages 64–65.
    NOTES: Thick coins will require a thicker material than mat board. Foam-core works well; however, it is difficult to get a clean cut on both sides.

    This type of mounting works well with many odd-shaped flat items.

2. Place coin on white mat board exactly where you want it to be. Trace the coin lightly with a hard-lead pencil.
    NOTE: Coin stores have acrylic cases that fit coins. Some of these are square on the outside, some are round. Either will work well. It is not necessary to use these cases, but they save time and create a neat, finished look.

3. Using a craft knife, cut a circle slightly smaller than traced line. Undercutting makes coin fit snugly in the hole.

6 Project

What you need to get started:

Tools:
- Basic framing tools (see pages 10–11)

Materials:
- Coin
- Double-sided tape
- Frame, ready-made or custom built
- Framing tape
- Glass
- Hanging hardware
- Kraft paper
- Mat board, white and one other color

A commemorative coin from the Prague National Theatre is elevated to the status of fine art when it is framed and specially mounted so both sides can be viewed. Size: 9½" x 9½"

NOTE: *A circle mat cutter will make a cleaner hole. This operation can be done at a professional frame shop, or you can purchase a circle mat cutter. The instructions for these cutters are easy to follow.*

4. Trace hole in the white mat onto back of colored mat.

   NOTE: *You can cut any shape of hole that you wish; however, for this project, we will cut a circle to give a uniform appearance to the display.*

5. Plot out circle onto back of colored mat ¼" larger than traced circle. Cut out circle.

6. Press coin into circle on white mat.

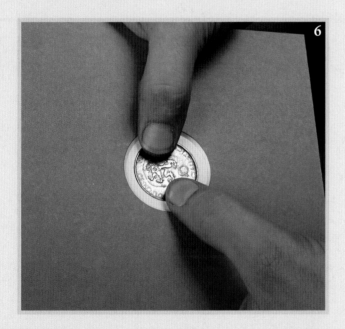

7. Adhere both mats together with double-sided tape.

8. Cut glass to size of mats. Refer to Cutting glass on pages 34–36.

9. Cut another piece of glass roughly 2" larger than the coin.

10. Place the smaller piece of glass over back of the coin and tape to reverse side of white mat.

Finishing the frame

1. Fit frame package into selected frame and secure. Refer to Frame finishing on page 30.

2. Cut a piece of kraft paper larger than frame. Cut a circle in kraft paper slightly larger than coin.

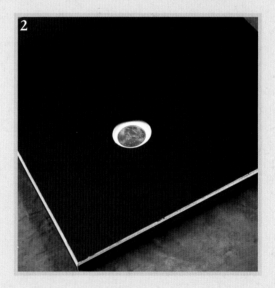

3. Center the hole in kraft paper over coin and attach paper to back of frame. Refer to Backing the frame on page 45.

4. Attach a sawtooth hanger. Refer to Attaching a sawtooth hanger on page 30.

7
Project

How do I surface–mount small thin objects?

Small objects can be tied, glued, or screwed into place in a frame.

What you need to get started:

Tools:
- Basic framing tools (see pages 10–11)
- Craft knife
- Hot-glue gun
- Needle
- Push pin

Materials:
- Double-sided tape
- Lightweight fishing line, clear
- Frame, ready-made or custom built
- Framing tape
- Glass
- Hanging hardware
- Hot-glue sticks
- Kraft paper
- Mat board
- Small object to be framed (watch)

Watch Shadow Box

Activity concepts: Making a small shadow box, securing a small object with fishing line.

For objects thinner than ½", there are an infinite number of framing possibilities. Small nonvaluable items can be glued down, but this project uses a less intrusive method of attachment.

Here's how:

1. Choose a mat as a backing for the item you want to frame.

2. This type of mounting requires a frame roughly 1½"–2" larger all around than the object.

3. Cut mat backing to size of rabbet opening plus ½". Refer to Assembling the shadow box on pages 58–59.

4. Draw four lines on back of mat ½" in from edges.

5. Using mat cutter, score cuts ½ of the way through mat, following lines, with the blade beveling toward center of mat.

6. Using a craft knife, cut out mat corners.

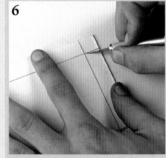